ROAD BIKE

The
Smokies

16 GREAT RIDES
IN NORTH CAROLINA'S
GREAT SMOKY MOUNTAINS

Jim Parham

Book design by Ron Roman
Cover photo by Mary Ellen Hammond

WMC Publishing, P.O. Box 158, Almond, NC 28702

Library of Congress Cataloging-In-Publication Data

Parham, Jim.
     Road bike the Smokies : 16 great rides in North Carolina's
Great Smoky Mountains / Jim Parham.
          p.   cm.
     ISBN 1-889596-02-7 (pbk.)
     1. Bicycle touring—Great Smoky Mountains (N.C. and
Tenn.)—Guidebooks. 2. Bicycle touring—North Carolina—
Guidebooks. 3. Great Smoky Mountains (N.C. and Tenn.)—
Guidebooks. 4. North Carolina—Guidebooks. I. Title.
GV1045.5.G78P37 1997
796.6'4'0976889—dc21   97-18741
                                                       CIP

Printed in the United States on recycled paper

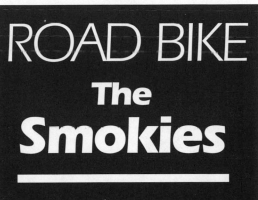

ROAD BIKE
The
Smokies

16 GREAT RIDES
IN NORTH CAROLINA'S
GREAT SMOKY MOUNTAINS

Jim Parham

WMC
Publishing

Almond, North Carolina

Contents

Introduction

North Carolina's beautiful Smoky Mountains lie in the far western corner of the state. Anchored by the Great Smoky Mountains National Park, the region encompasses a diverse landscape of rolling farmland, quiet valleys, deep river gorges and rugged mountains. Its residents live in small towns with picturesque old domed courthouses, in tiny Appalachian communities, on rambling mountain farms and tucked away in hidden coves. Throughout the area, connecting all these people to the rest of the world, you'll find a network of roads ideal for cycling.

This guide describes 16 of the best road bike rides in the North Carolina Smokies. Road biking here is as good as it gets. The roads themselves are smoothly paved and kept in good condition, and most of them see very light motor traffic. Even stretches of the four-lane highways are good for cycling. The Blue Ridge Parkway, the Cherohala Skyway and the Mountain Waters Scenic Byway are all here, along with lesser known backroads like Burningtown, Yellow Creek and Alarka. The variety of terrain covered on these roads is remarkable.

This region offers great riding for all ability levels, and these rides should appeal to most any rider on most any kind of bike. Several large rivers traverse the area, creating broad, flat valleys where the roads tend to meander and roll over small hills, perfect for cyclists seeking less challenging routes. In sharp contrast to the valleys are the rugged mountains that surround them. Individuals looking for the most demanding rides will head straight up into the hills where elevations top out at close to 6000 feet. What you'll find the most of, though, are routes of moderate difficulty that connect the valleys. These rides have a little bit of everything—climbs, descents and stretches where you can spin to your heart's delight.

It's possible to ride on the roads of the Smokies year-round, but the most consistently good riding days are in spring, summer and fall. Each season brings something different. Springtime is glorious, with wildflowers blooming in abundance. There's nothing quite like riding on a warm, breezy April day when the trees are glowing nearly neon green with new leaves. Expect cool mornings followed by warm afternoons and evenings with low humidity. You'll see the fewest cars at this time of year.

As summer rolls around, things begin to heat up and more tourists are on the roads. In peak summer, midday can be hot and humid, and short afternoon thundershowers are not uncommon. Mornings and evenings are still quite pleasant. If you're on the road before 10 a.m. you'll encounter the fewest cars, even on the busiest roads.

Fall weather starts sometime in September and can last until early December. These are the bright, clear, warm, low-humidity days excellent for outdoor excursions. Beginning in October, the trees put on a brilliant color show and the mountainsides are splashed with reds, yellows, oranges, greens and browns. This is also a time to be extra cautious of leaf peeping motorists who tend to watch the trees as much as they watch the roadway.

As you use this book to pick your route, you'll want to pay close attention to several things. Most important is the overall mileage and the elevation profile. Picking a route that's too long, has too much climbing, or both, can turn a nice day into grueling nightmare. Also, take a look at the general time allowance for your ability level. Remember too that riding in unfamiliar territory where you're making frequent stops to check the map and directions always takes a bit longer than you would guess. Many of these rides pass by country stores or through small towns somewhere along the route. However, some are quite remote and are noted as such. Carry plenty of liquids and nourishment with you so as not to run out far from "civilization."

If you need a bike shop for assistance, repairs or supplies, there are four in the area. You'll find their names, addresses and phone numbers on page 9. Tourism is the region's biggest industry, so finding lodging, camping and dining establishments is not a problem. If you plan to stay overnight, it's a good idea to book lodging ahead. County Chambers of Commerce (also listed on page 9) can provide you with information on available accommodations.

Road biking in the North Carolina Smokies can be as good a time as you'll ever have on a bike, and this guide is intended to lead you to the finest the area has to offer. Stuff it in a baggie and stick it in your pocket, or just carry a copy of the map and detailed directions for your chosen route. Then hit the pavement for some of the best road riding of your life.

J.P.
June, 1997

Rules of the Road

The bicycle has legally been considered a vehicle in North Carolina since 1937. Thus bicyclists have full rights and responsibilities on the roadway and are subject to the regulations governing the operation of a motor vehicle, where applicable.

North Carolina traffic laws require the rider of a bicycle to:
- Ride on the right, in the same direction as other moving traffic
- Obey all traffic signs and signals, including stop and yield signs and one-way directional signs
- Use signals to communicate intended movements
- Yield to pedestrians and emergency vehicles
- For night riding, equip the bicycle with a front lamp visible from 300 feet and a rear reflector or lamp which is visible from a distance of 200 feet at night

To insure a safe trip:
- Always wear a bicycle helmet
- Carry plenty of liquids
- Avoid biking at night
- When riding with a group, ride single file
- Wear bright clothing to increase visibility
- Be sure your bicycle is the right size for you and keep it in good repair, checking for loose or worn parts regularly

Remember, the bicyclist always loses in a conflict with a motor vehicle. Ride defensively and in a predictable manner to avoid accidents. Be courteous to other drivers. Keep traffic flowing by helping motorists pass you in a safe manner.

Bike Shops

Nantahala Gorge

Nantahala Outdoor Center
Bike Shop
13077 Hwy 19W
Bryson City, NC 28713
704/488-2175

Sylva

Motion Makers
17 E Main Street
Sylva, NC 28779
704/586-6925

Cherokee

Queen's Trading Post
US 441N
Cherokee, NC 28719
704/497-4453

Franklin

Smoky Mountain Bicycles
West Palmer Street
Franklin, NC 28734
704/524-1238

Chambers of Commerce

Bryson City

Bryson City Chamber
P.O. Box 509
Bryson City, NC 28713
704/488-3681 or 800/867-9249

Franklin

Franklin Chamber
425 Porter Street
Franklin, NC 28734
704/524-3161 or 800/336-7829

Cherokee

Cherokee Visitors Center
P.O. Box 460
Cherokee, NC 28719
704/497-9195 or 800/438-1601

Robbinsville

Graham County Chamber
P.O. Box 1206
Robbinsville, NC 28771
704/479-3790 or 800/470-3790

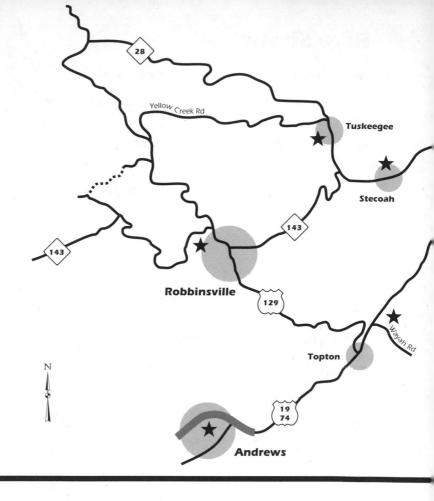

The area locator map above serves as a general reference to all the starting points in this book. Start locations are marked with a star ★. For turn-by-turn directions and a detailed map of a specific ride, refer to the individual route description.

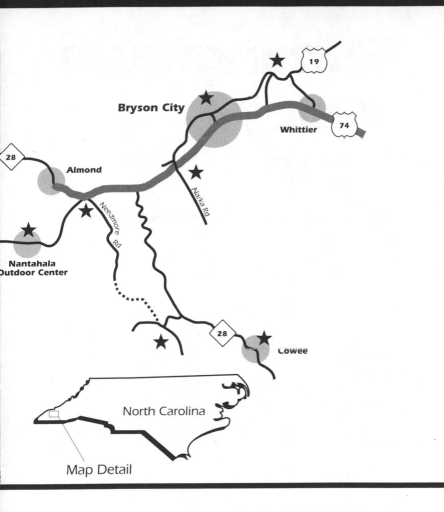

Bryson City

Whittier

Almond

Nantahala Outdoor Center

Natka Rd

Needmore Rd

Cowee

North Carolina

Map Detail

Burningtown Valley Loop

Rating: Easy   19 Miles

This ride is rated easy because of its length combined with the fact that there are few climbs along the route.

A local favorite, this ride loops through the valley formed by Burningtown Creek and the Little Tennessee River. High mountains loom on either side, but the valley itself is relatively flat—one of the reasons for its popularity. It's also quite beautiful. You'll roll through pastoral scenery past rambling mountain farms and alongside the creek and the river. Look carefully and you might even detect the remains of an old Indian fish trap in the Little Tennessee. Keep an eye out for underwater, V-shaped rock formations in the shoals.

Estimated Riding Times
- Beginner: 2.5 - 3 hours
- Intermediate: 1.5 - 2 hours
- Advanced: 1 - 1.25 hours

Directions to the Start
- Ride begins at the junction of Lower Burningtown Creek Road and Tellico Road. Just pull off in the grass beside the road.
- From the junction of US 19/74, NC 28 and Needmore Road, take Needmore Road 9 miles. Turn left on Tellico Road and go 0.3 miles to the start.

Alternate Start: Lost Bridge at the junction of NC 28 and Tellico Road.

Ride Characteristics & Cautions
- Most of route follows quiet country roads
- NC 28 is not a heavily used highway but motorists do tend to move along at a good clip
- Watch for barking and chasing dogs at a few of the farm houses

Points of Interest
- Little Tennessee River
- Ancient Fish Traps
- Old iron bridge across Little Tennessee
- Side trip to Cowee Valley

Burningtown Valley Loop

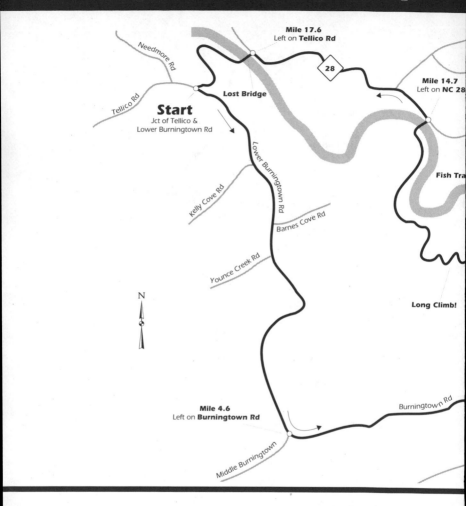

Mile 17.6
Left on **Tellico Rd**

Needmore Rd

28

Mile 14.7
Left on **NC 28**

Tellico Rd

Lost Bridge

Start
Jct of Tellico &
Lower Burningtown Rd

Kelly Cove Rd

Lower Burningtown Rd

Barnes Cove Rd

Younce Creek Rd

Fish Tra

N

Long Climb!

Mile 4.6
Left on **Burningtown Rd**

Burningtown Rd

Middle Burningtown

Profile

2000'

1000'   0.0

Ber

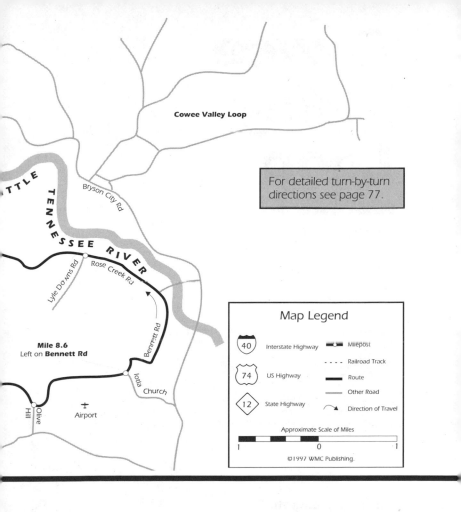

Cowee Valley Loop

TTLE

TENNESSEE RIVER

Bryson City Rd

For detailed turn-by-turn directions see page 77.

Lyle Downs Rd

Rose Creek Rd

Bennett Rd

Mile 8.6
Left on **Bennett Rd**

Iota
Church

Hill

Olive

✈ Airport

Map Legend

40	Interstate Highway		Milepost
		---	---
			Railroad Track
74	US Highway		Route
			Other Road
12	State Highway		Direction of Travel

Approximate Scale of Miles

1   0   1

©1997 WMC Publishing.

Hill Rd

Little Tennesee River

9.0

18.5

Cowee Valley Loop

Rating: Easy   8 Miles

This ride is rated easy because of its short length. There are several short but steep hills.

Gem mines and lots of them. That's what you will see on this route. The Cowee Valley is renowned for its precious stones, and the mines are a main tourist attraction. The mine supplies the dirt and a sluice, and you supply the labor to see what you find. Kids (and rockhounds, of course) love it! You'll also pass by Perry's Water Gardens which has free tours, and the Cowee Creek Pottery—all in a beautiful mountain valley with very little traffic.

Estimated Riding Times
- Beginner: 1 - 2 hours
- Intermediate: 0.5 - 1 hour
- Advanced: 0.5 hours

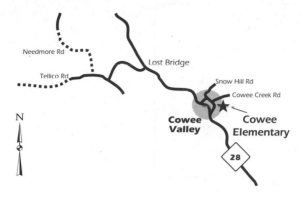

Directions to the Start
- Ride begins at Cowee Elementary School on Cowee Creek Road, just off NC 28 part way between Franklin and Bryson City in the Cowee Valley.

Ride Characteristics & Cautions
- Entire ride is on rural backroads
- There are 2 half-mile climbs on the route. One starts at milepost 2.9 and the other starts at milepost 5.9. Each has a short but steep descent.
- It's not uncommon to see loose dogs on this route

Points of Interest
- Gem mines
- Perry's Water Gardens (open Mon.-Sat:. 9-12 & 1-5, Sun: 1-5) Free admission
- Cowee Creek Pottery (just off route)
- Snow Hill Inn Bed & Breakfast

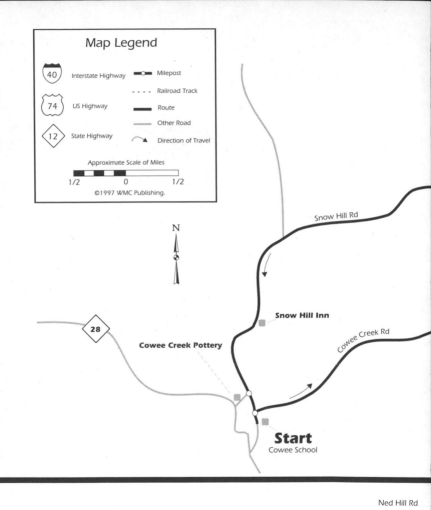

Map Legend

40 Interstate Highway
74 US Highway
12 State Highway

Milepost
Railroad Track
Route
Other Road
Direction of Travel

Approximate Scale of Miles
1/2   0   1/2
©1997 WMC Publishing.

N

28

Snow Hill Rd

Snow Hill Inn

Cowee Creek Pottery

Cowee Creek Rd

Start
Cowee School

Ned Hill Rd

Profile
2000'
1000'   0.0

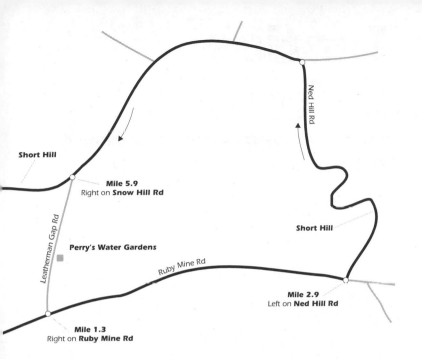

Short Hill

Mile 5.9
Right on **Snow Hill Rd**

Leatherman Gap Rd

Ned Hill Rd

Short Hill

Perry's Water Gardens

Ruby Mine Rd

Mile 2.9
Left on **Ned Hill Rd**

Mile 1.3
Right on **Ruby Mine Rd**

For detailed turn-by-turn directions see page 77.

Snow Hill Rd

4.0

8.3

Tootie's Cafe

Rating: Easy   9 Miles

This ride is rated easy because of its short distance. There are two short climbs.

Tootie's Cafe is located in the heart of the small mountain community of Stecoah and it is where you will start and end this ride. It's a classic backroads diner complete with the big EAT sign right out front. The ride itself follows first Stecoah Creek and then Sawyer's Creek through scenic rural farmland. There are several interesting barns and a good number of cows en route. You'll climb two moderate hills, one halfway out on the loop and the other just before the end, making for a fast downhill finish. Be sure to stop in the Cafe before or after your ride and get a bite to eat.

Estimated Riding Times
- Beginner: 1 hour
- Intermediate: 45 minutes
- Advanced: 30 minutes

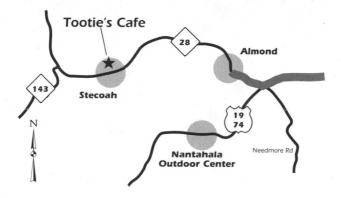

Directions to the Start
- Ride starts at Tootie's Cafe.
- Tootie's Cafe is located on NC Highway 28 in Stecoah. Look for the big EAT sign out front.

Ride Characteristics & Cautions
- The last 3 miles of the route follow NC Highway 28 which most of the time has fairly light traffic. However, do be cautious of logging and other large trucks. They tend to drive pretty fast and have a reputation for not giving cyclists much room.
- Watch for loose gravel in the roadway on the first descent at milepost 3.5.
- Check your speed on the last descent down into Stecoah. It's not too hard to go upwards of 40 m.p.h.

Points of Interest
- Tootie's Cafe itself
- Interesting barns

Tootie's Cafe

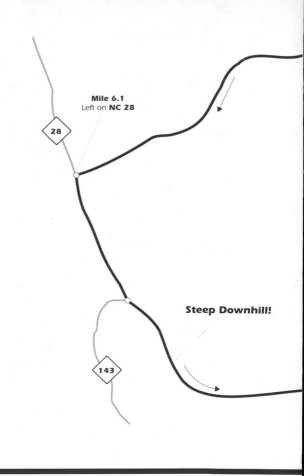

Mile 6.1
Left on **NC 28**

28

Steep Downhill!

N

143

Profile

Lower Stecoah Rd

2000'

1000' 0.0

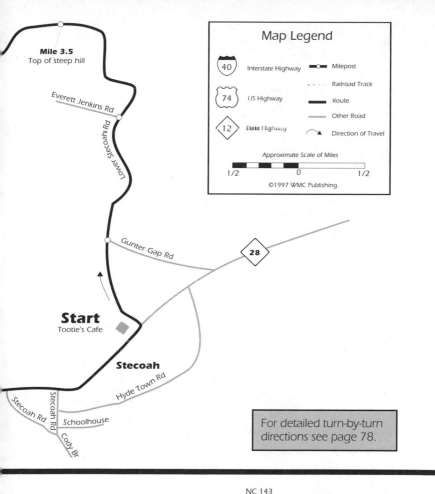

Map Legend

(40) Interstate Highway	●━━●━ Milepost
(74) US Highway	─ ─ ─ ─ Railroad Track
(12) State Highway	━━━ Route
	━━━ Other Road
	➤ Direction of Travel

Approximate Scale of Miles

1/2   0   1/2

©1997 WMC Publishing.

Mile 3.5
Top of steep hill

Everett Jenkins Rd

Lower Stecoah Rd

Gunter Gap Rd

28

Start
Tootie's Cafe

Stecoah

Hyde Town Rd

Stecoah Rd

Stecoah Rd

Schoolhouse

Cody Br

For detailed turn-by-turn directions see page 78.

NC 143

5.0   9.1

23

Valley River Loop

Rating: Easy   15 Miles

This ride is rated easy because of its short length and relatively flat terrain.

The Valley River valley between Andrews and Murphy is broad and flat with towering mountains on either side. This fertile area is filled with farms. On this ride you'll pass horse farms, cattle farms and large corn fields as well as a small mountain airport. Starting at a convenient rest area on the eastern edge of Andrews, you'll pass right through this small town before heading out alongside the meandering Valley River. At the community of Marble, you'll cross over the river and to the other side of the four-lane to return.

Estimated Riding Times
- Beginner: 1.5 - 2 hours
- Intermediate: 1 - 1.5 hours
- Advanced: 1 hour or less

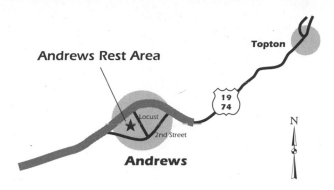

Andrews Rest Area

Topton

Locust

2nd Street

Andrews

N

Directions to the Start
- Ride begins at the rest area on US 19/74 just east of Andrews

Ride Characteristics & Cautions
- Passes through downtown Andrews, a very small town
- There is little shade on this route, so be prepared with sunscreen
- There are no major hills, but you do roll up and down a fair amount at the beginning of the ride

Points of Interest
- Valley River
- Downtown Andrews shops
- Andrews/Murphy Airport
- Cattle and horse farms, big cornfields

Valley River Loop

For detailed turn-by-turn directions see page 78.

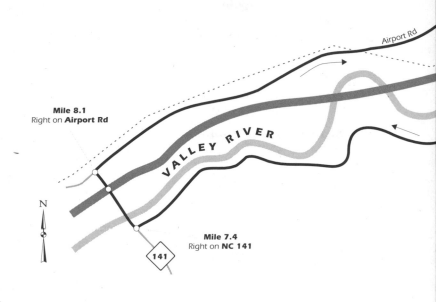

Airport Rd

Mile 8.1
Right on **Airport Rd**

VALLEY RIVER

N

Mile 7.4
Right on **NC 141**

141

Profile

2000'

1000'

0.0

Fairview Rd

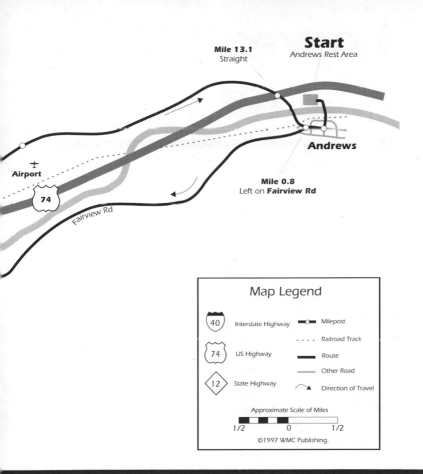

Start
Andrews Rest Area

Mile 13.1
Straight

Andrews

Mile 0.8
Left on **Fairview Rd**

+
Airport

74

Fairview Rd

Map Legend

40 Interstate Highway   ●━○ Milepost

             - - - - Railroad Track

74 US Highway   ▬▬ Route

             ▬▬ Other Road

12 State Highway   ⌒▲ Direction of Travel

Approximate Scale of Miles

1/2   0   1/2

©1997 WMC Publishing.

US 19/74

7.0

14.5

Lower Alarka

Rating: Moderate
13 Miles

This ride is rated moderate due to two tough hills, each with a tricky descent.

This route lies on a hilly wedge of land bordered on three sides by water. On one side is the Tuckaseegee River and on the other is Alarka Creek. The far end is capped off by Fontana Lake. The flattest section of the entire route is right at the beginning as you cross the bridge over the four-lane. After that, it's nonstop up one little hill and down another, with plenty of curves on each. Halfway through the ride you'll make a two-mile climb which leads into a fun roller coaster ride out to the shores of Lake Fontana. You'll pass two waterfalls, a small one that falls almost in the road, and another along Alarka Creek. To double the length of this ride, combine it with the Upper Alarka route.

Estimated Riding Times
- Beginner: 2 hours
- Intermediate: 1.25 hours
- Advanced: 45 minutes

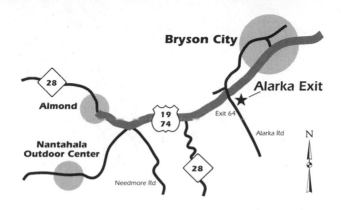

Directions to the Start
- Ride begins at junction of US 19, US 74 and Alarka Road. Take Exit 64 off US 74.
- Park at the dirt pull-off on the south side of the 4-lane.

Ride Characteristics & Cautions
- Route follows narrow rural roads for its entirety
- Use caution on the downhills, some have tight turns and gravel tends to wash into the road after rain storms
- There are numerous barking dogs along this route; some are chained, some are not

Points of Interest
- Lake Fontana
- Waterfalls
- Side trip to the spring at Cold Springs Baptist Church

Lower Alarka

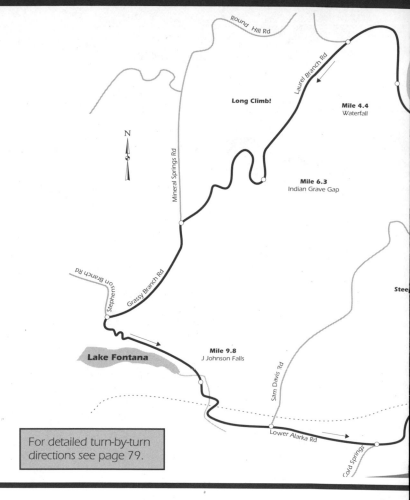

Round Hill Rd

Laurel Branch Rd

Long Climb!

Mile 4.4
Waterfall

N

Mineral Springs Rd

Mile 6.3
Indian Grave Gap

on Branch Rd

Stephens

Grassy Branch Rd

Steep

Lake Fontana

Mile 9.8
J Johnson Falls

Sam Davis Rd

For detailed turn-by-turn directions see page 79.

Lower Alarka Rd

Cold Springs

Profile

Robinson Gap Rd

2000'

1000'

0.0

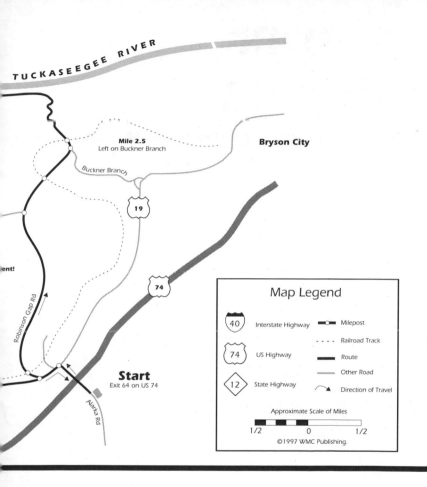

TUCKASEEGEE RIVER

Mile 2.5
Left on Buckner Branch

Bryson City

Buckner Branch

19

74

ent!

Robinson Gap Rd

Start
Exit 64 on US 74

Narka Rd

Map Legend

40 Interstate Highway   •—• Milepost

                         - - - - Railroad Track

74 US Highway   ▬▬ Route

                            Other Road

12 State Highway   ⌒▲ Direction of Travel

Approximate Scale of Miles

1/2   0   1/2

©1997 WMC Publishing.

ndian Grave Gap

0   12.9

Upper Alarka

Rating: Moderate   15 Miles

This ride is rated moderate due to one very steep and long hill, with a very fast descent.

The Upper Alarka valley is one of the most beautiful around. It begins with a gradual twisting climb to high, open pasturages. You'll then head into a steep climb that takes you to Deep Gap. For the majority of the ride you'll follow alongside Alarka Creek, a small but lively stream. At some points the road is so close to the creek you can feel the cool air drifting up from the spray of the rapids. The farther you go up the valley, the narrower the road gets, as if you're being squeezed by the mountains. By the time you reach the top of the climb, the road is hardly more than a single lane. Take care on the descent down Deep Gap Road; it's often washed over with gravel.

Estimated Riding Times
- Beginner: 2.5 hours
- Intermediate: 1.5 hours
- Advanced: 1 hour

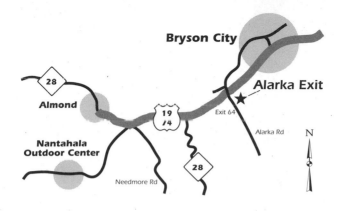

Directions to the Start
- Ride begins at the junction of US 19, US 74 and Alarka Road. Take Exit 64 off US 74.
- Park at the dirt pull-off on the south side of the 4-lane.

Ride Characteristics & Cautions
- Route follows narrow rural roads for its entirety
- Use caution on the downhill on Deep Gap Road, as gravel tends to wash into the road after rain storms
- Watch for loose dogs in the roadway
- The upper portion of Alarka Road is very narrow. Watch for cars coming down the hill toward you.

Points of Interest
- Scenic Valley
- Trout stream
- Views on Deep Gap Road
- Friendly people

Upper Alarka

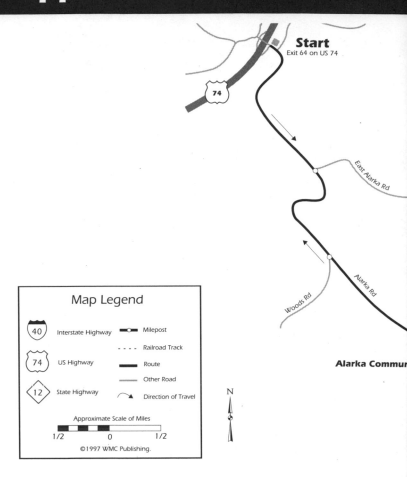

Start
Exit 64 on US 74

74

East Alarka Rd

Alarka Rd

Woods Rd

Alarka Commu

Map Legend

40 Interstate Highway ⬤━ Milepost

- - - - Railroad Track

74 US Highway ━━━ Route

Other Road

12 State Highway Direction of Travel

N

Approximate Scale of Miles

1/2   0   1/2

©1997 WMC Publishing.

Profile

3000'

2000'

1000' 0.0

For detailed turn-by-turn
directions see page 80.

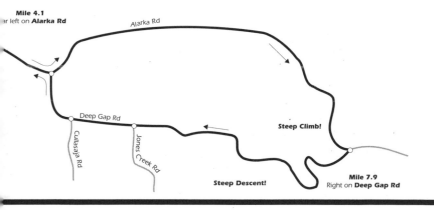

Mile 4.1
ar left on **Alarka Rd**

Alarka Rd

Deep Gap Rd

Cullasaja Rd

Jones Creek Rd

Steep Climb!

Steep Descent!

Mile 7.9
Right on **Deep Gap Rd**

Deep Gap

8.0   14.8

Whittier Loop

Rating: Moderate   21 Miles

This ride is rated moderate due to the consistently rolling hills, as well as two sections on a four-lane highway.

Almost every Wednesday evening in the summertime you'll find a number of local riders out on the Whittier Loop for their weekly training ride. They've chosen this route because of its long flat stretches which are good for spinning and because there are no major climbs to break up the group. But it's not just a good training ride, it's a good ride, period. You'll cruise alongside the Tuckaseegee River and through lovely rolling farmland laced with white fences. You'll also ride right through the small village of Whittier.

Estimated Riding Times
- Beginner: 2 - 3 hours
- Intermediate: 1.5 - 2 hours
- Advanced: 1+ hour

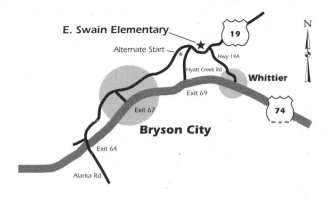

Directions to the Start
- Ride begins at East Swain Elementary School
- Take Ela exit 69 off US 74 and take Hyatt Creek Road to US 19
- Turn right on US 19 and proceed to E Swain Elementary

Alternate Start: if school is in session, turn right on US 19 and start at the River Launch parking area just down the road

Ride Characteristics & Cautions
- You'll start and finish on a short section of US 19, a 2-lane road which is a very popular tourist route. Watch for traffic.
- US 441 is the main route into Cherokee. It's a 4-lane and has no shoulder, but it does have a curb—no escape!
- Watch your speed on the downhill on Sunset Farm Road. It's steep and ends abruptly at 4-lane US 74.

Points of Interest
- Tuckaseegee River
- Rolling farmland and mountain views
- Cherokee Indian Reservation is very nearby, although riding into downtown Cherokee during tourist season is not recommended

Whittier Loop

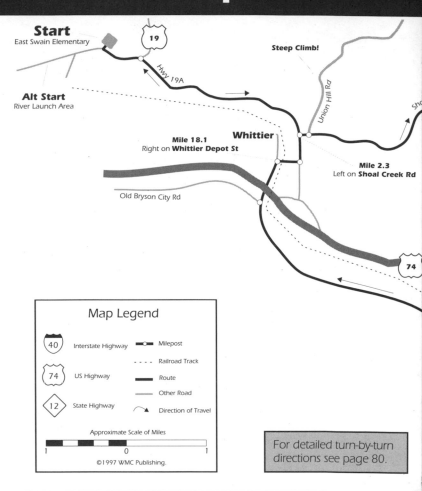

Start
East Swain Elementary

19

Hwy 19A

Steep Climb!

Union Hill Rd

Alt Start
River Launch Area

Mile 18.1
Right on **Whittier Depot St**

Whittier

Mile 2.3
Left on **Shoal Creek Rd**

Old Bryson City Rd

74

Map Legend

40 — Interstate Highway
●—● Milepost

74 — US Highway
- - - - Railroad Track
━━━ Route
──── Other Road

12 — State Highway
◠▲ Direction of Travel

Approximate Scale of Miles

1   0   1

©1997 WMC Publishing.

For detailed turn-by-turn directions see page 80.

Profile

2000'

1000' 0.0

Olivet Church Rd

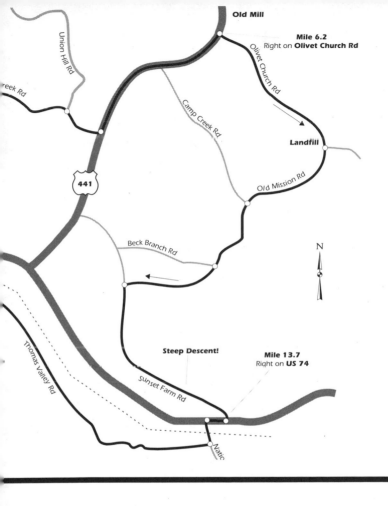

Old Mill

Mile 6.2
Right on **Olivet Church Rd**

Union Hill Rd

Olivet Church Rd

Creek Rd

Camp Creek Rd

Landfill

441

Old Mission Rd

Beck Branch Rd

N

Thomas Valley Rd

Steep Descent!

Mile 13.7
Right on **US 74**

Sunset Farm Rd

Natic

Sunset Farm Rd

10.0

20.8

Road to Nowhere

Rating: Moderate   17 Miles

This ride is rated moderate mainly due to the number and length of the uphills.

This is the locally famous "Road to Nowhere," a road leading into the Great Smoky Mountains National Park that was begun in 1941 and has yet to be completed. It was intended to connect Bryson City to Fontana Dam via the north shore of Lake Fontana, and would have enabled local citizens to easily visit the old home places and gravesites lost to them upon completion of the dam and designation of the National Park. The project was dropped long ago and many folks are still bitter about it, which explains the sign on your left just before you enter the Park. It does lead somewhere, however—to several trail heads and a long, dark tunnel that's fun to walk through. The road itself makes a great road bike route. It sees none of the congested traffic typical in the rest of the Park, and the scenery is just as spectacular.

Estimated Riding Times
- Beginner: 2.5 - 3 hours
- Intermediate: 2 hours
- Advanced: 1 - 1.25 hours

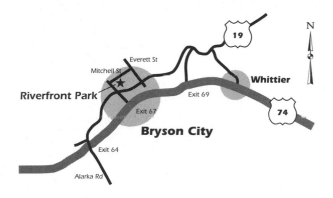

Directions to the Start
- Ride begins at Riverfront Park in Bryson City
- The park is right beside the county courthouse on Mitchell Street and shares the same parking lot
- Park in the spaces closest to Riverfront Park sign

Ride Characteristics & Cautions
- All but 3 miles of this ride are in the Great Smoky Mountains National Park
- Use caution on the descent down to Noland Creek after milepost 6.2; it's steep and long
- You'll pass Swain County High School at milepost 1.4. When school is in session, students tend to drive with reckless abandon when leaving school between the hours of 3 and 4 p.m.
- No riding is allowed off the paved road within the National Park

Points of Interest
- Great Smoky Mountains National Park
- Tunnel
- Overlook and Quiet Walkway at milepost 6.2

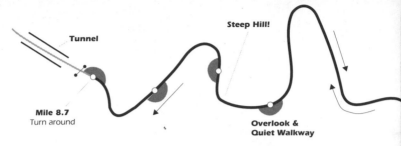

Great Smoky Mountains National Park

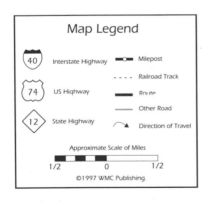

Map Legend

(40)	Interstate Highway	●—○—	Milepost
(74)	US Highway	- - - -	Railroad Track
		▬▬▬	Route
(12)	State Highway	▬▬▬	Other Road
		⌒➤	Direction of Travel

Approximate Scale of Miles

1/2   0   1/2

©1997 WMC Publishing.

TUCKAS

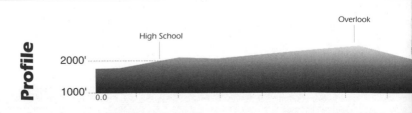

For detailed turn-by-turn
directions see page 81.

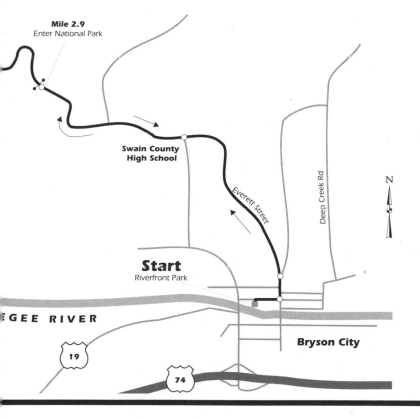

Mile 2.9
Enter National Park

**Swain County
High School**

Everett Street

Deep Creek Rd

N

Start
Riverfront Park

EGEE RIVER

Bryson City

19

74

Tunnel

Overlook

High School

9.0

17.4

28/ Needmore

Rating: Moderate   23 Miles

This ride is rated moderate due to the steep rolling hills combined with a section of dirt road.

On this route, you'll ride up one side of the Little Tennessee River and back down the other. You can think of Highway 28 as the high road (lots of good views) and Needmore as the low road (alongside the river). Highway 28 is renowned for its twists and curves and numerous short ups and downs. It's a lot of fun and typically hasn't much traffic. Once on Needmore, things flatten out considerably as much of it is level with the river. In fact, sometimes the wide river and its splashing shoals are only a few feet away.

Special note: A four-mile section alongside the Little Tennessee River follows a dirt road. Most of the time this road is very hard-packed and fine for a road bike. However, if the road has recently been graded or it's springtime "mud season," you're in for a rough ride.

Estimated Riding Times
- Beginner: 2 - 3 hours
- Intermediate: 1.5 - 2 hours
- Advanced: 1 -1.5 hours

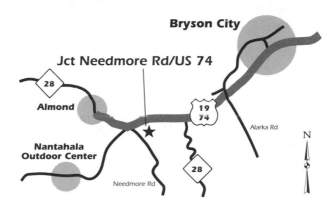

Directions to the Start
- Ride begins at the junction of US 19/74, NC 28 and Needmore Road
- Park at the grass pull-off used by commuters at the bottom of Needmore Road just before it intersects with US 19/74

Ride Characteristics & Cautions
- First 3 miles of route follow 4-lane US 19/74. It has a good shoulder and not much traffic
- There are some fast downhill curves on Highway 28. Use caution at high speeds and stay in your lane
- Although the dirt section of Needmore Road sees light traffic, it is frequently used as a shortcut by local residents travelling to and from Franklin. These folks know the road well and some may be driving faster than they should. Stay well to your side of the road. Skinny tires do not react as quickly on hard-packed gravel as they do on pavement.

Points of Interest
- Little Tennessee River
- Honor system honey stand
- Lost Bridge

28/Needmore

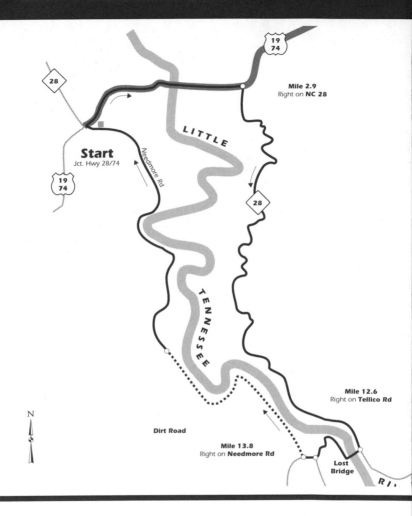

Start
Jct. Hwy 28/74

Needmore Rd

LITTLE

TENNESSEE

Mile 2.9
Right on **NC 28**

Mile 12.6
Right on **Tellico Rd**

Mile 13.8
Right on **Needmore Rd**

Lost
Bridge

Dirt Road

N

Profile

Hwy 28

2000'

1000'   0.0

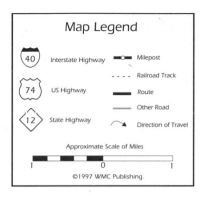

Map Legend

$\boxed{40}$ Interstate Highway   ▬●▬ Milepost

- - - - Railroad Track

$\boxed{74}$ US Highway   ▬▬ Route

              Other Road

$\langle 12 \rangle$ State Highway   ➤ Direction of Travel

Approximate Scale of Miles

1   0   1

©1997 WMC Publishing.

For detailed turn-by-turn directions see page 82.

Little Tennesee River

12.0

22.8

Robbinsville Loop

Rating: Moderate/Difficult   45 Miles

This ride is rated moderate/difficult due to its length and the number of long sustained climbs.

Starting from the Nantahala Outdoor Center Bike Shop and ending through the beautiful Nantahala Gorge, this ride takes you through some incredible countryside. The route is best known for its long climbs and harrowing experiences near Robbinsville, the community that gives it its name. It seems everyone who has done this ride several times or more can recall being honked at or yelled at, has had a close encounter with a semi, or some worse experience near its infamous namesake. Nevertheless, it's a great ride, complete with astounding views, torturous climbs and exhilarating descents.

Estimated Riding Times
- Beginner: not recommended
- Intermediate: 3 - 3.5 hours
- Advanced: 2.5 hours

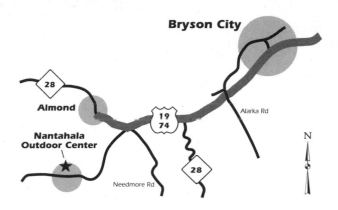

Directions to the Start
- Ride begins at the Nantahala Outdoor Center Bike Shop
- NOC is located 15 miles west of Bryson City on US 19/74
- Park on other side of river, across the steel bridge

Ride Characteristics & Cautions
- Use caution on US 19/74 through the Nantahala Gorge. This road sees a lot of tourist traffic during the summer season, especially on weekends.
- **Tip:** an early morning start is the best way to avoid the tourist traffic on most any day
- There are 4 really long climbs on this route
- 80% of the ride is on state or US 2-lane highways

Points of Interest
- Nantahala Gorge whitewater rafting
- Stecoah Gap Appalachian Trail crossing
- Some really neat barns

Robbinsville Loop

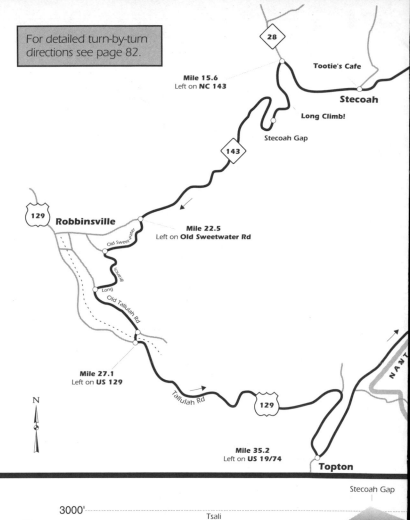

For detailed turn-by-turn directions see page 82.

28

Tootie's Cafe

Mile 15.6
Left on **NC 143**

Stecoah

Long Climb!

Stecoah Gap

143

129 **Robbinsville**

Old Sweetwater

Mile 22.5
Left on **Old Sweetwater Rd**

Branch

Long

Old Tallulah Rd

Mile 27.1
Left on **US 129**

N

Tallulah Rd

129

NANT

Mile 35.2
Left on **US 19/74**

Topton

Profile

Stecoah Gap

3000'

Tsali

2000'

1000' 0.0

50

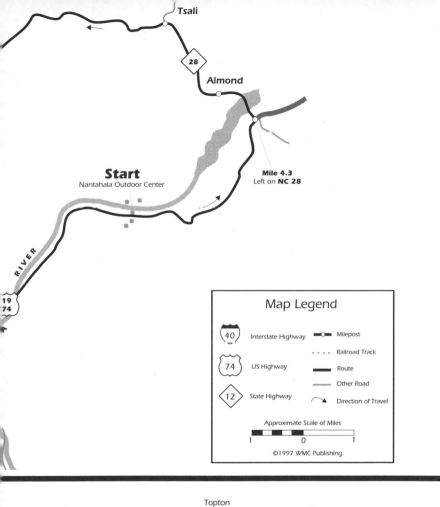

Tsali

28

Almond

Start
Nantahala Outdoor Center

Mile 4.3
Left on **NC 28**

RIVER

19
74

Map Legend

40 Interstate Highway — ● — Milepost

74 US Highway ---- Railroad Track

12 State Highway ━━ Route

⌢ Other Road

↗ Direction of Travel

Approximate Scale of Miles

1   0   1

©1997 WMC Publishing.

Topton

22.0   45.0

Seven Eleven

Rating: Moderate/Difficult   41 Miles

This ride is rated moderate or difficult depending on where you start. It's difficult if you start at the Nantahala Launch Site because you'll begin with an almost continuous 20-mile climb. It's moderate if you skip half the hill and use the alternate start.

You'll start out with one heck of a long climb on this route. Fortunately it's very gradual and tempered by the sight-seeing you get to do on the way up. Just down the road from the start you'll pass so close to an old power house you can almost feel the charge of electricity as you pass by. Soak up what you can for the climb ahead. As you follow the course of the upper Nantahala River you'll pass waterfall after waterfall. One section is known as the "cascades." Farther up, and once on the gated Forest Service Route 711 (no traffic here), the views of the surrounding peaks are simply stunning. It's like riding on a private Blue Ridge Parkway. After a few rolling ridges, you'll start the long, swooping descent down to the shores of Lake Nantahala and finally back along the river, reversing the long climb with an easy coast.

Estimated Riding Times
- Beginner: shorter route recommended
- Intermediate: 5 - 5.5 hours
- Advanced: 3.5 - 4 hours

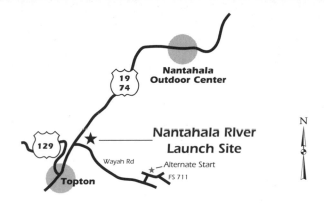

Directions to the Start
- Ride begins at Nantahala River Launch Site on US 19/74
- Use of the parking area requires a parking fee
- There are changing and rest room facilities here

Alternate Start: To shorten the ride and much of the first hill, you may want to start at the beginning of Forest Service 711.

Ride Characteristics & Cautions
- Ride characterized by a very long climb and a long descent
- Route includes one very short section of hard-packed dirt road just before Forest Service Route 711
- Forest Service 711 is gated on both ends and the gates remain closed most all of the year. This means there will be no traffic, and you must be prepared to be entirely self-sufficient in case of emergency.
- **Caution:** The downhill curves on Forest Service 711 can have patches of loose gravel
- **Caution:** The far gate on Forest Service 711 is at the bottom of a long, steep hill. It comes up very fast.

Points of Interest
- Old Nantahala Power & Light power house
- Cascades of Nantahala River
- Overlooks on Forest Service 711
- Lake Nantahala
- Bartram Trail crossing

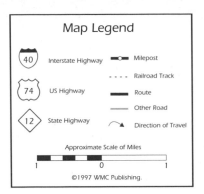

Map Legend

(40) Interstate Highway   ●— Milepost

                         - - - - Railroad Track

(74) US Highway   ▬▬ Route

                         ═══ Other Road

⟨12⟩ State Highway   ⌒▲ Direction of Travel

Approximate Scale of Miles

1   0   1

©1997 WMC Publishing.

For detailed turn-by-turn directions see page 83.

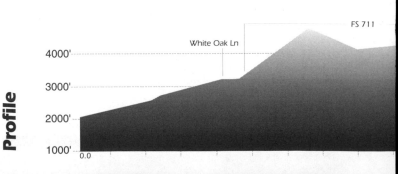

FS 711

White Oak Ln

4000'

3000'

Profile

2000'

54

1000'

0.0

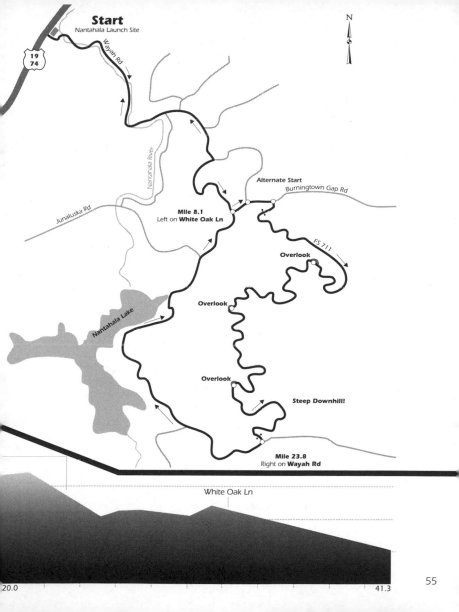

Start
Nantahala Launch Site

19 74

Wayah Rd

Nantahala River

Junaluska Rd

Alternate Start

Burningtown Gap Rd

Mile 8.1
Left on **White Oak Ln**

FS 711

Overlook

Overlook

Nantahala Lake

Overlook

Steep Downhill!

Mile 23.8
Right on **Wayah Rd**

N

White Oak Ln

20.0

41.3

Brasstown Loop

Rating: Moderate/Difficult   45 Miles

This ride is rated moderate/difficult mainly due to its length.

This is one of the westernmost rides you can do in North Carolina. Considering its length, it's surprising there are no major climbs on the route. The reason: you'll be taking advantage of a broad valley where two rivers, the Hiwassee and the Valley River, come together. Starting in Andrews, you'll ride all the way to Brasstown, famous as the location of the John C. Campbell Folk School. The school focuses on Appalachian crafts, performing arts and agriculture. This ride takes you right through the school, and its large complex of buildings makes it a great place to stop for a break. You'll take in downtown Andrews twice and downtown Murphy once, but for the most part you'll be in very rural farm country. In fact, at one point you'll nearly ride right through a Holstein cattle barn.

Estimated Riding Times
- Beginner: 4 - 6 hours
- Intermediate: 3 - 4 hours
- Advanced: 2.5 - 3 hours

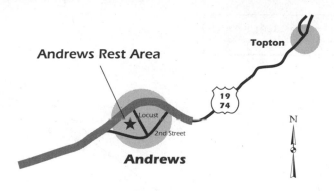

Andrews Rest Area

Topton

Locust

2nd Street

Andrews

N

Directions to the Start
- Ride begins at the rest area on US 19/74, just east of Andrews.

Ride Characteristics & Cautions
- Much of ride is on backcountry roads, but does pass through downtown Murphy (a small town) and downtown Andrews (an even smaller town)
- There are long stretches of road with little or no shade, so be prepared with sunscreen
- Follow the directions carefully enough to avoid riding on 4-lane US 19/74—a busy road
- Use caution just before entering Murphy. There are some sharp switchbacks on a short but steep hill.

Points of Interest
- Valley River
- Cattle and horse farms
- John C. Campbell Folk School

Brasstown Loop

For detailed turn-by-turn directions see page 84.

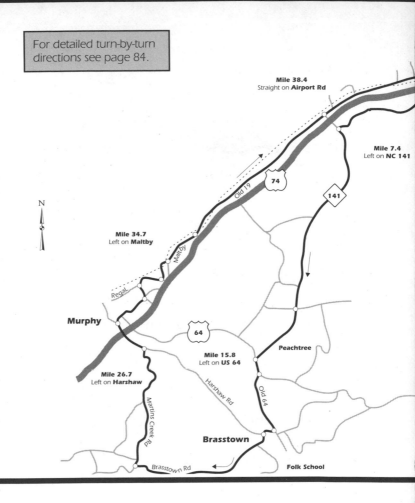

Mile 38.4
Straight on **Airport Rd**

Mile 7.4
Left on **NC 141**

74 · Old 19

141

N

Mile 34.7
Left on **Maltby**

Maltby

Regal

Murphy

64

Mile 15.8
Left on **US 64**

Peachtree

Mile 26.7
Left on **Harshaw**

Harshaw Rd

Old 64

Martins Creek Rd

Brasstown

Brasstown Rd

Folk School

Profile

2000'

Fairview Rd

John C. Campbell Fo

1000'   0.0

58

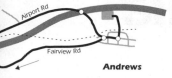

Start
Andrews Rest Area

Airport Rd

Fairview Rd

Andrews

Mile 0.8
Left on **Fairview Rd**

Map Legend

(40)	Interstate Highway	●━●	Milepost
(74)	US Highway	- - - -	Railroad Track
		━━━	Route
(12)	State Highway	———	Other Road
		⌒▲	Direction of Travel

Approximate Scale of Miles

1   0   1   2

©1997 WMC Publishing.

Murphy

22.0   44.8

Cherohala Skyway

Rating: Difficult   54 Miles

This ride is rated difficult due to its overall length, the extreme elevation gained and the length and grade of both the uphills and downhills.

A truly epic ride. You can make this route shorter depending on where you choose to start, but no matter where you begin, it's still epic. From Lake Santeetla you'll gain 3400 feet in a continuous 11-mile climb, most of which is a 9% grade. The views are the best around and rivaled only by the Blue Ridge Parkway. There are 12 pull-offs on the Skyway itself before you reach the Tennessee state line. You can see all of the Great Smoky Mountains National Park, the Joyce Kilmer-Slickrock Wilderness, Lake Santeetla, and from the state line the Tennessee River and the Cumberland Plateau—it's amazing. This road is brand new and smooth as silk; the downhills are very fast. The state line sits atop the ridge before a really long downhill, so if you decide to continue on into Tennessee, be prepared for a long climb back up.

Estimated Riding Times
- Beginner: not recommended
- Intermediate: 4 - 6 hours
- Advanced: 3 - 4 hours

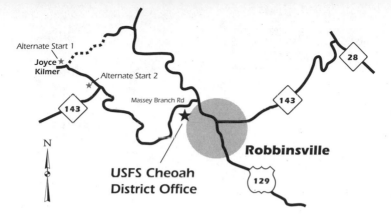

Directions to the Start
- Ride begins at the Forest Service Cheoah Ranger Station outside of Robbinsville.
- Take US 129 north out of town and turn left on Massey Branch Road (NC 143). It's one mile to the ranger station on the left.

Alternate Start 1: Joyce Kilmer Memorial Forest parking area, 2.5 miles past entrance to Cherohala Skyway

Alternate Start 2: Picnic table pull-off 0.5 miles past entrance to Cherohala Skyway

Ride Characteristics & Cautions
- Entire ride is on 2-lane winding mountain roads
- NC 143 is curvy and rolling as it follows Lake Santeetla before the entrance to the Skyway
- Make sure your brakes are in top-notch working order. 11 downhill miles at 9% grade can put a lot of wear on your pads
- Watch your speed on the downhills. Motorists may be watching the views and not for you
- Carry provisions and water; there is little or none en route
- It can get really foggy, really windy and much cooler in the higher elevations of this ride. Avoid rainy days.

Points of Interest
- Lake Santeetla
- Joyce Kilmer Memorial Forest—a short hike through big trees
- Views, views and more views

Cherohala Skyway

For detailed turn-by-turn directions see page 85.

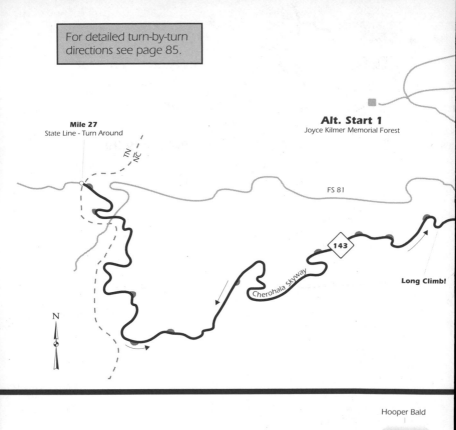

Mile 27
State Line - Turn Around

TN
NC

Alt. Start 1
Joyce Kilmer Memorial Forest

FS 81

143

Cherohala Skyway

Long Climb!

N

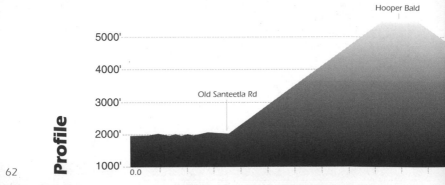

Hooper Bald

5000'

4000'

3000'

Old Santeetla Rd

2000'

Profile

1000'

0.0

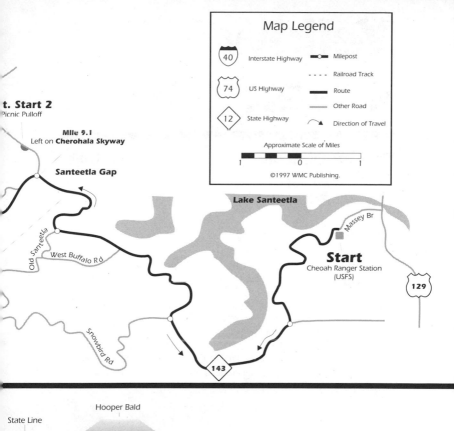

Map Legend

40	Interstate Highway	●━━●	Milepost
74	US Highway	- - - -	Railroad Track
12	State Highway	━━━━	Route
		━━━━	Other Road
		◣	Direction of Travel

Approximate Scale of Miles

1   0   1

©1997 WMC Publishing.

t. Start 2
Picnic Pulloff

Mile 9.1
Left on **Cherohala Skyway**

Santeetla Gap

Old Santeetla

West Buffalo Rd

Snowbird Rd

Lake Santeetla

Massey Br

Start
Cheoah Ranger Station
(USFS)

129

143

State Line

Hooper Bald

Old Santeetla Rd

26.0

54.0

Yellow Creek

Rating: Difficult   38 Miles

This ride is rated difficult mainly due to the climbs, one of which is arguably the steepest paved climb in North Carolina.

It's hard to think of the Yellow Creek ride without getting obsessed by the hill climb up to Yellow Creek Gap. It's very, very steep and can turn even the strongest set of legs into jello. The funny thing is, it's only a small portion of the route, yet it seems to linger in your thoughts and come up in conversation the entire time. Nevertheless, this is a wonderful ride. You'll follow the road high above Lake Fontana and then along the western edge of the Great Smoky Mountains National Park, right beside Lake Cheoah. Many waterfalls cascade out of the Park and into the lake. The second half of the ride follows the Cheoah River and Yellow Creek itself. The big climb is almost at the end. Look for a dazzling display of wildflowers in spring.

Estimated Riding Times
- Beginner: not recommended
- Intermediate: 3 - 4 hours
- Advanced: 2 hours

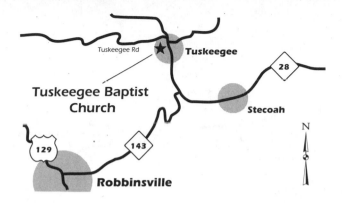

Directions to the Start
- Ride begins at Tuskeegee Baptist Church on NC 28 or (when church is in session) at Tuskeegee Motel just down the road

Ride Characteristics & Cautions
- Make sure your brakes are in tip-top shape. The descent down Yellow Creek is steeper than the climb up.
- There are a lot of climbs and descents on this route
- Watch your speed coming down Yellow Creek. There are driveways toward the bottom and cars may be pulling out.
- There are only a couple of stores along the route, one at Fontana Village and one at Deal's Gap

Points of Interest.
- Fontana Dam (highest in the East). You'll ride right past the base of it and you can take a short side trip to the top.
- Great Smoky Mountains National Park
- Cheoah Dam (a scene from *The Fugitive* was filmed here)
- Water diversion projects
- A lot of neat barns
- Trout farm
- Cross Appalachian Trail twice

Yellow Creek

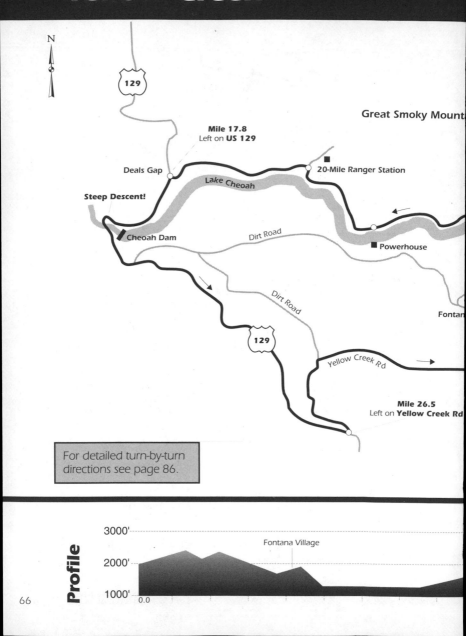

N

129

Great Smoky Mount

Mile 17.8
Left on **US 129**

Deals Gap

Lake Cheoah

20-Mile Ranger Station

Steep Descent!

Cheoah Dam

Dirt Road

Powerhouse

Dirt Road

129

Fontan

Yellow Creek Rd

Mile 26.5
Left on **Yellow Creek Rd**

For detailed turn-by-turn directions see page 86.

Profile

3000'

Fontana Village

2000'

1000'

0.0

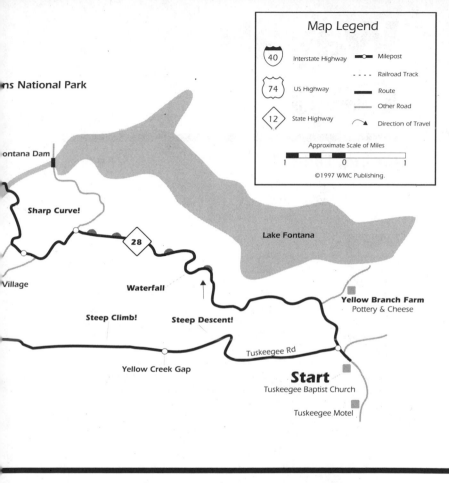

Map Legend

(40) Interstate Highway		●—● Milepost	
(74) US Highway		- - - Railroad Track	
<12> State Highway		Route	
		Other Road	
		Direction of Travel	

Approximate Scale of Miles

1   0   1

©1997 WMC Publishing.

ns National Park

ontana Dam

Sharp Curve!

Lake Fontana

28

Village

Waterfall

Steep Climb!   **Steep Descent!**

Yellow Branch Farm
Pottery & Cheese

Yellow Creek Gap   Tuskeegee Rd

Start
Tuskeegee Baptist Church

Tuskeegee Motel

Yellow Creek Gap

Below Cheoah Dam

20.0   38.4

Wayah Gap

Rating: Difficult   70 Miles

This ride is rated difficult due to the overall length as well as the climbs on NC 28 and the very long climb up to Wayah Gap.

Much of this ride is along the Mountain Waters Scenic Byway, a series of roads following beautiful rivers and streams in western North Carolina. You'll see a lot of waterfalls. It also follows portions of the Mountains-to-Sea state bike route. Starting at the Nantahala Outdoor Center, you'll ride all the way to Franklin on the very curvy and hilly NC Highway 28—a real roller coaster ride. Leaving Franklin, the climb up to Wayah Gap is long and torturous as well as beautiful. The road follows a cool rushing stream the entire way up. Your reward for the climb: 27 miles of almost continuous downhill! You'll pass by Lake Nantahala, the Cascades of the Upper Nantahala River and through the Nantahala Gorge. What a way to finish.

Estimated Riding Times
- Beginner: not recommended
- Intermediate: 6 - 7 hours
- Advanced: 4 - 5 hours

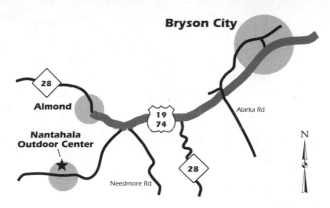

Directions to the Start

- Ride begins at the Nantahala Outdoor Center Bike Shop on US 19/74 in the Nantahala Gorge
- Park in the far parking lots across the steel bridge on the other side of the river

Ride Characteristics & Cautions

- US 19/74 through the Nantahala Gorge sees a lot of tourist traffic as well as truck traffic
- You'll follow a 4-lane highway for 3 miles. It has a wide shoulder.
- NC 28 has quite a few blind curves. Be sure to stay well to the right side of the road.
- There is a convenience store at the turn onto Wayah Road. It's the last place of its kind for a long way.
- You'll find water at Arrowood Glades Campground. This is a good place to tank up before beginning the long climb.
- There's plenty of shade on this route

Points of Interest

- Nantahala River rafting and Nantahala Outdoor Center (they have a good bike shop and three restaurants)
- Cowee Pottery
- Fresh produce stands and an honor system honey stand
- Gem mines
- Lots of waterfalls

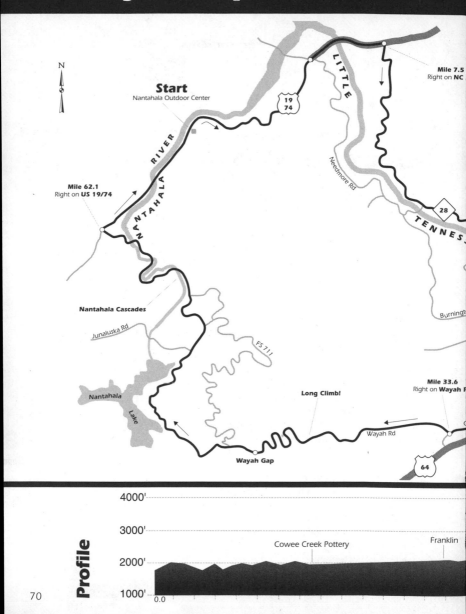

N

Start
Nantahala Outdoor Center

Mile 7.5
Right on **NC**

19 74

LITTLE

Needmore Rd

Mile 62.1
Right on **US 19/74**

28

TENNES

NANTAHALA RIVER

Nantahala Cascades

Burningt

Junaluska Rd

FS 711

Long Climb!

Mile 33.6
Right on **Wayah R**

Nantahala
Lake

Wayah Rd

Wayah Gap

64

Profile

4000'

3000'

Cowee Creek Pottery

Franklin

2000'

1000'

0.0

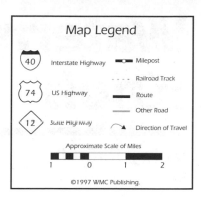

Map Legend

(40)	Interstate Highway	●━━●	Milepost
		- - - -	Railroad Track
(74)	US Highway	▬▬▬	Route
		▬▬▬	Other Road
(12)	State Highway	⌒ ▲	Direction of Travel

Approximate Scale of Miles

1　　0　　1　　2

©1997 WMC Publishing.

Cowee Creek Pottery

Murphy Rd　　Franklin

For detailed turn-by-turn directions see page 87.

Wayah Gap

36.0　　　　　　　　　　　　　　　　　70.1

Waterrock Knob

Rating: Difficult   63 Miles

This ride is rated difficult due to its overall length and the extreme elevation gain.

Half of this route uses the last 26 miles of the famous Blue Ridge Parkway, where you'll climb to the top of Waterrock Knob at an elevation of 5800 feet—the highest elevation reached in this book. The other half is as diverse as it gets. You'll travel through quiet valley farmland, along a wide-shouldered four-lane highway, up a short section of dirt road and through the heavily congested tourist town of Cherokee. It's a real mixed bag and its a great ride. The views from the Parkway are simply stunning. There's a long downhill through six tunnels that's a blast, and beating the traffic through Cherokee is a true challenge. Give yourself plenty of time to enjoy this one.

Estimated Riding Times
- Beginner: not recommended
- Intermediate: 6 - 7 hours
- Advanced: 4 - 5 hours

Directions to the Start
- Ride begins at East Swain Elementary School
- Take Ela exit 69 off US 74 and take Hyatt Creek Road to US 19
- Turn right on US 19 and proceed to E Swain Elementary

Alternate Start: if school is in session, turn right on US 19 and start at the River Launch parking area just down the road

Ride Characteristics & Cautions
- Use caution on the one mile of 4-lane US 441. There's no shoulder, but there's a curb—no escape.
- US 74 is a 4-lane highway. It has a wide shoulder—use it.
- There is a 2-mile stretch of hard-packed dirt road on the climb to Balsam Gap. It's the best way to avoid the 4-lane, but if you can't stand the thought of dirt, use the 4-lane.
- Weather conditions can be quite different (cooler, foggy, etc.) at the high elevations on the Parkway. Be prepared.
- When riding through the Blue Ridge Parkway tunnels, use of a front light and rear reflector is required by law. It's also a very good idea. The tunnels are pretty dark. Don't forget these items.
- US 19 leaving Cherokee is 2-lane, narrow and quite busy with tourist traffic

Points of Interest
- Balsam Mountain Inn
- Overlooks, views and tunnels on the Blue Ridge Parkway
- Cherokee gift shops and the Museum of the Cherokee Indian

Waterrock Knob

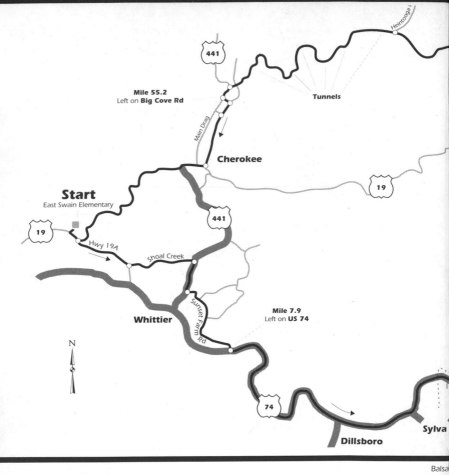

441

Mile 55.2
Left on **Big Cove Rd**

Main Drag

Tunnels

Heintooga

Cherokee

19

Start
East Swain Elementary

19

Hwy 19A

Shoal Creek

441

Mile 7.9
Left on **US 74**

Sunset Farm Rd

Whittier

N

74

Dillsboro

Sylva

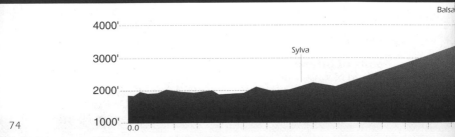

Balsa

4000'

3000'

Sylva

2000'

1000' 0.0

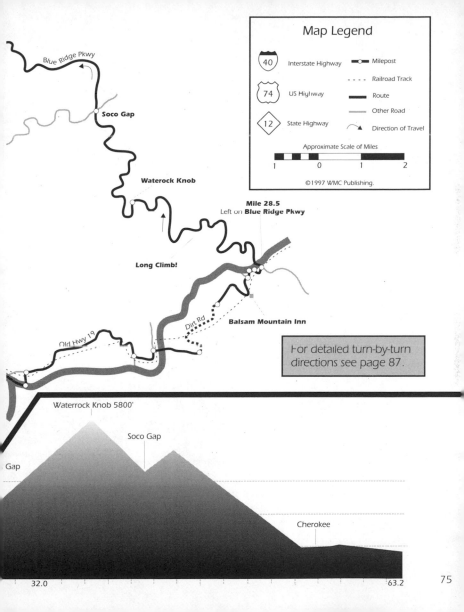

Map Legend

(40)	Interstate Highway	●—○	Milepost
(74)	US Highway	- - - -	Railroad Track
(12)	State Highway	▬▬	Route
		➤	Other Road
		➤	Direction of Travel

Approximate Scale of Miles

©1997 WMC Publishing.

Blue Ridge Pkwy

Soco Gap

Waterock Knob

Mile 28.5
Left on **Blue Ridge Pkwy**

Long Climb!

Old Hwy 19

Dirt Rd

Balsam Mountain Inn

For detailed turn-by-turn directions see page 87.

Waterrock Knob 5800'

Soco Gap

Gap

Cherokee

32.0   63.2

Burningtown Valley Loop (p. 12)

0.0	↑	Ride **straight** onto Lower Burningtown Road. Much of this route follows Bike Route 35 and some of Bike Route 30.
1.9	↑	Continue **straight**. Barnes Cove Road enters from the left.
3.8	↑	Continue **straight**. Younce Creek Road enters from the right.
4.6	↖	Bear **left** on Burningtown Road. Middle Burningtown Road bears off to the right.
7.3	↑	Continue **straight**. Olive Hill Road (Bike Route 30) enters from the right.
8.6	↰	Turn **left** on Bennett Hill Road.
9.5	↰	Turn **left** on Rose Creek Road.
10.0	↑	Continue **straight**. Lyle Downs Road enters from the left.
14.7	↰ (STOP)	Cross Little Tennessee River on old iron bridge and turn **left** on NC 28 (Bryson City Road).
17.6	↰	Turn **left** across Lost Bridge on Tellico Road.
18.5		Finish.

Cowee Valley Loop (p. 16)

0.0	↱	Turn **right** to exit Cowee School onto Cowee Creek Road. Much of this ride follows Bike Route 36.
0.1	↗	Bear **right** to remain on Cowee Creek Road.
1.3	↗	Bear **right** on Ruby Mine Road. The entrance to Perry's Water Gardens is 0.4 miles to the left down Leatherman Gap Road.
2.9	↰	Turn **left** on Ned Hill Road. Start a half-mile climb.
3.5	↑	Top of climb. Continue **straight**.
4.5	↰ (STOP)	Turn **left** on Leatherman Gap Road.
5.9	↱	Turn **right** on Snow Hill Road. The entrance to Perry's Water Gardens is 0.4 miles straight down Leatherman Gap Road.
7.7	↑	Continue **straight** past Snow Hill Inn B & B.

Cowee Valley Loop (continued)

8.0 ↑ Continue **straight**. Cowee Creek Pottery is just down road to the right.

8.2 ↱(STOP) Turn **right** at the stop sign on Cowee Creek Road.

8.3 ↰ Turn **left** to finish at Cowee School.

Tootie's Cafe (p. 20)

0.0 Leave Tootie's Cafe on Lower Stecoah Road

0.8 ⌐ Bear **left** to stay on Lower Stecoah Road.

2.2 ↑ Continue **straight**, Everett Jenkins Road enters from the left.

3.5 ↑ Top of steep hill. Continue **straight** and begin downhill switchbacks.

6.1 ↰ Turn **left** on NC Highway 28 and begin climb.

7.3 ↑ Top of climb. NC Highway 143 exits to the right. Stay **straight** and begin a rather long and steep downhill.

9.1 ↰ Turn **left** to finish at Tootie's Cafe.

Valley River Loop (p. 24)

0.0 Leave rest area on entrance road.

0.1 ↱(STOP) Turn **right** at stop sign on Locust Street.

0.4 ⬚ **Caution:** cross railroad tracks.

0.5 ↱🚦 At traffic light, turn **right** on 2nd Street.

0.8 ↰ Turn **left** on Fairview Road at bank building and before crossing railroad tracks.

0.9 ↗ Bear **right** to remain on Fairview Road.

7.4 ↱ Turn **right** on NC 141 and cross Valley River.

7.7 ↑🚦 Cross 4-lane US 19/74 under traffic light and **straight** onto Marble Road.

8.1 ↱(STOP) Turn **right** at stop sign on Airport Road.

10.1 ⬚ **Caution:** cross tracks.

11.9	↑	Pass Murphy/Andrews Airport.
13.1	↑▢	Cross 4-lane US 19/74 under traffic light and continue **straight** into town of Andrews on 2nd Street.
13.8	⧄	**Caution:** cross railroad tracks.
13.9	↑	Continue **straight** past Fairview Road.
14.1	◀▢	Turn **left** at traffic light on Locust Street.
14.2	⧄	**Caution:** cross tracks.
14.5	◀	Turn left into rest area to finish.

Lower Alarka (p. 28)

0.0		Leave pull-out onto Alarka Road and cross 4-lane US 19/74 on bridge.
0.2	◀	Turn **left** on Lower Alarka Road.
0.4	▶	Turn **right** on Robinson Gap Road.
0.5	⧄	**Caution:** cross railroad tracks.
1.9	↗	Bear **right** to remain on Robinson Gap Road.
2.3	⧄	**Caution:** cross railroad tracks.
2.5	◀	Turn **left** on Buckner Branch Road.
2.6	⧄	**Caution:** cross railroad tracks.
4.4	↑	Pass small waterfall on left.
4.8	↖	Bear **left** on Laurel Branch Road.
6.3	↑	Indian Grave Gap and top of long climb.
7.3	↑	Mineral Springs Road enters from the right. You are now on Grassy Branch Road.
8.3	↑	Stephenson Branch Road enters from right.
9.8	↑	Pass J Johnson Falls on left.
11.3	↑	Sam Davis Road enters on left. You are now on Lower Alarka Road.
11.6	↑▽	Continue **straight** at yield sign. Cold Springs Road enters from the right.
12.7	▶	Turn **right** on Alarka Road and cross 4-lane US 19/74 on bridge.
12.9		Finish at pull-out on left.

Upper Alarka (p. 32)

0.0		Leave pull-out onto Alarka Road and ride away from 4-lane US 19/74.
1.5	↑	Continue **straight**. East Alarka Road enters from the left.
4.1	⤙	Bear **left** to remain on Lower Alarka Road.
7.9	⮌	Turn sharply back to the **right** on Deep Gap Road and continue to climb.
8.2	↑	Deep Gap and top of climb.
8.7	↑	Jones Creek Road enters from left. Continue **straight**.
10.5	↑	Cullasaja Road enters from left. Continue **straight**.
10.7	⬅🛑	Turn **left** at stop sign onto Alarka Road and finish the way you came in.
14.8		Finish at pull-out.

Whittier Loop (p. 36)

0.0	⬅🛑	Leave East Elementary and turn left on US 19.
0.7	⤙	Turn **right** on Highway 19A and cross river.
2.3	⬅	Turn **left** on Shoal Creek Road.
2.6	↑	Continue **straight**. Union Hill Road enters from the left. If you want to add a good hill climb to this route, turn here. It enters back into route at mile 4.5.
4.5	↑	Union Hill Road reenters route on left.
4.6	⬅🛑	Turn **left** at stop sign on 4-lane US 441.
6.2	⤙	Turn **right** on Olivet Church Road.
8.0	⮎🛑	At stop sign just past the landfill, turn **right** on Old Mission Road.
9.4	⤙▽	At yield sign, bear **left** on Camp Creek Road.
10.8	↑	Beck Branch enters from the right. Continue **straight**.
12.2	⬅🛑	Turn **left** at stop sign on Sunset Farm Road.
13.7	⮎🛑	At bottom of steep hill, turn **right** on 4-lane US 74.
13.8	⬅	Turn **left** and back onto Nations Creek Road.
13.8+	▨	**Caution:** cross railroad tracks.

13.9	⊩	Turn **right** on Thomas Valley Road.
18.1	⊩	Cross under US 74 and turn **right** on Whittier Depot Street.
18.1+	⬓	**Caution:** cross railroad tracks.
18.2	⬅STOP	Turn **left** at stop sign on Highway 19A.
18.5	↑	Pass Shoal Creek Road.
20.1	⅄STOP	Turn **left** at Lloyd's Motor Court onto US 19.
20.8	⊩	Finish at East Swain Elementary.

Road to Nowhere (p. 40)

0.0	⊩STOP	Leave Riverfront Park and turn **right** onto Mitchell Street.
0.1	⬅	Turn **left** onto Everett Street at traffic light.
0.2	⬓	**Caution:** cross railroad tracks.
0.3	⅄	Bear **left** up the hill to remain on Everett Street.
1.4	↑	Pass Swain County High School.
2.9	↑	Pass through gate into Great Smoky Mountains National Park.
6.2	↑	Pass overlook and quiet walkway on the left. Start steep downhill.
8.1	↑	Bottom of steep downhill. Pass trailhead parking area on the left.
8.4	↑	Pass trailhead parking area on the left.
8.7	↑	Trailhead parking area and gate. Just beyond the gate is a tunnel. On the other side of the tunnel, the road ends. Turn around here and go back the way you came. **Note:** riding in the tunnel is not recommended due to almost total darkness and broken glass.
17.4	⊣	Finish at Riverfront Park.

Highway 28/Needmore Road (p. 44)

0.0		Leave pull-out at junction of US 19/74 and Needmore Road, and ride up hill on 4-lane US 19/74.
2.9	⮕	At Texaco Station, turn **right** on NC Highway 28 (Bryson City Road). This is a very hilly and curvy road.
12.6	⮕	Turn **right** across Lost Bridge and Little Tennessee River onto Tellico Road.
13.5	⬈	Bear **right** to remain on Tellico Road. Lower Burningtown Road enters from the left.
13.8	⮕	Turn **right** onto Needmore Road. **Caution:** this is a hard-packed dirt road for the next 3.2 miles.
17.0	↑	Roadway becomes paved again.
22.8	🛑	Finish down steep hill at junction of Needmore Road and US 19/74.

Robbinsville Loop (p. 48)

0.0		Leave Nantahala Outdoor Center and ride east on US 19/74. **Caution:** this road has no shoulder and can be busy during the tourist season.
4.3	⬅	Just before US 19/74 turns to 4-lane, turn **left** on NC 28. **Caution:** you may encounter construction on parts of this road as it is being widened to 4-lane.
6.2	↑	Pass through community of Almond.
7.8	↑	Pass entrance to Tsali Recreation Area (great mountain biking).
14.2	↑	Pass through community of Stecoah. This is the bottom of the long climb to Stecoah Gap.
15.6	⬅	Turn **left** on NC 143 and continue to climb.
17.4	↑	Stecoah Gap and top of climb. The Appalachian Trail crosses here.
22.5	⬅	Turn **left** on Old Sweetwater Road.

23.9	◄┤	Turn **left** on Long Branch Road. This is a hidden turn.
25.2	←▽	Turn **left** on Old Tallulah Road at yield sign.
26.4	├►	Turn **right** across small bridge to remain on Old Tallulah Road.
27.1	←⊗	Turn **left** at stop sign on US 129 (Tallulah Road).
35.2	←⊗	Turn **left** at stop sign on US 19/74 down the hill and into the Nantahala Gorge.
37.3	↑	Pass launch site for Nantahala River (whitewater rafting).
40	↑	Pass Ferebee Memorial Park.
45	◄┤	Finish at Nantahala Outdoor Center.

Seven Eleven (p. 52))

0.0		Leave Nantahala Launch Site and ride up alongside the Upper Nantahala River on Wayah Road. There are many beautiful waterfalls on this river.
8.1	◄┤	Turn **left** on White Oak Lane.
8.3	┬►	Turn **right** onto Burningtown Gap Road. **Caution:** the next 0.4 miles are on a hard-packed dirt road.
8.7	├►	Turn right on Forest Service Road #711. This is a paved road, but look for loose gravel in the roadway.
13.1	↑	Pass overlook on the right.
16.9	↑	Pass overlook on the right.
21.2	↑	Pass overlook on right and begin the long downhill back to the start. Cross Bartram Trail.
23.8	┬►	Turn **right** on Wayah Road. **Caution:** there is a gate just before this turn. To avoid being clotheslined, don't carry too much speed down the hill.
33.2	↑	Pass White Oak Lane on right.
41.3	├►	Finish at Nantahala Launch Site.

Brasstown Loop (p. 56)

0.0		Leave rest area on entrance road.
0.1	↱(STOP)	Turn **right** on Locust Street.
0.4	⬊	**Caution:** cross railroad tracks.
0.5	↱🚦	At traffic light, turn **right** on 2nd Street.
0.8	↰	Turn **left** on Fairview Road at bank building and before crossing railroad tracks.
0.9	↗	Bear **right** to remain on Fairview Road.
7.4	↰(STOP)	Turn **left** on NC 141. This follows NC Bike Route 2 (Mountains-to-Sea Route).
13.2	↑	Pass through community of Peachtree.
15.8	↰(STOP)	Turn **left** at stop sign on US 64.
16.4	↦	Turn **right** on Old 64.
17.3	↦	Turn **right** on Brasstown Road at Clay's Corner Store.
17.7	↑	Pass through campus of John C. Campbell Folk School.
22.2	↱(STOP)	Turn **right** on Martins Creek Road.
26.7	↰(STOP)	Turn **left** at stop sign on Harshaw Road.
27.3	↑🚦	Cross 4-lane US 19/74 at traffic light onto Hiwassee Street.
28.2	↑🚦	Continue **straight** at traffic light past Macon County courthouse. The road becomes Valley River Avenue and then Hill Street.
30.2	↰(STOP)	Pass shopping centers, then turn **left** at 4-way stop sign.
30.6	↦	Turn **right** just before railroad tracks on Regal Road.
31.6	↰	Turn **left** just before 4-lane on Old Tomatla Road.
32.7	⬊	**Caution**: cross railroad tracks.
32.9	⬊	**Caution**: cross railroad tracks.
33.0	↰	Turn **left** on Tomatla Road.
34.7	↰⬊	Turn sharply to the **left** to avoid the 4-lane and cross the railroad tracks on Maltby Road.
36.4	⬊↰	**Caution:** cross railroad tracks, then turn **left** on Old 19.
38.4	↑	Pass **straight** through community of Marble and continue on what is now Airport Road.
40.4	⬊	**Caution**: cross tracks.
42.2	↑	Pass Murphy/Andrews Airport.

43.4   ↑▯   Cross 4-lane US 19/74 under traffic light and continue **straight** into town of Andrews on 2nd Street.

44.1   ⟍   **Caution:** cross railroad tracks.

44.2   ↑   Continue **straight** past Fairview Road.

44.4   ←▯   Turn **left** at traffic light on Locust Street.

44.5   ⟍   **Caution:** cross tracks.

44.8   ←   Turn left into rest area to finish.

Cherohala Skyway (p. 60)

0.0   Leave US Forest Service Cheoah Ranger District Office and ride west on NC 143.

2.3   ↱(STOP)   Turn **right** at stop sign to remain on NC 143.

4.5   ↑   Continue straight. Snowbird Road enters from the left.

7.6   ↑   Old Santeetla Road enters from the left. This is the start of an 11-mile climb!

9.1   ←   Santeetla Gap. Elevation 2660 feet. Turn **left** to begin the Cherohala Skyway. You are still on NC 143.

11.1   ↑   First overlook.

12.3   ↑   Shute Cove overlook. Elevation 3550 feet.

13.1   ↑   Third overlook.

14.7   ↑   Fourth overlook.

17.6   ↑   Spirit Ridge overlook. Elevation 4950 feet.

18.4   ↑   Top of long climb. Elevation 5400 feet.

19.4   ↑   Hooper Bald overlook. Elevation 5290 feet.

20.1   ↑   Santeetla Overlook. Elevation 5390 feet.

20.9   ↑   Big Junction overlook. Elevation 5240 feet.

22.1   ↑   Haw Knob overlook. Elevation 4890 feet.

25.2   ↑   Stratton Meadows. Forest Service Road #81 enters here. Elevation 4320 feet.

27.0   ∩   Tennessee/North Carolina State Line. Beech Gap. Elevation 4490 feet. Turn around here and go back the way you came.

54.0   ⊢   Finish at ranger station.

Yellow Creek (p. 64)

0.0		Leave Tuskeegee Baptist Church and ride north on NC 28.
0.2	↑	Continue **straight**. Tuskeegee Road enters from the left.
2.1	↑	Pass picnic table pull-off on right.
2.4	↑	Top of climb. Pass small waterfall on cliff to right.
4.2	↑	Pass picnic table pull-off on right.
5.1	↑	Pass Hazel Creek pull-off on right.
6.5	↑	Pass picnic table pull-off on right.
6.9	↑	Cross Appalachian Trail.
7.2	←(STOP)	Turn **left** to remain on NC 28 at stop sign. (Turn right here to tour top of Fontana Dam.)
8.8	↑	Pass through Fontana Village.
9.7	↑	**Caution:** dangerous downhill curve.
9.8	↑	Cross Little Tennessee River just below Fontana Dam.
13.2	↑	Pass powerhouse. It's just across Lake Cheoah.
14.9	↑	Great Smoky Mountains Twenty–Mile Ranger Station is just up road to the right.
17.8	←(STOP)	Deals Gap. Turn **left** at stop sign on US 129.
19.8	↑	Cross Little Tennessee River just below Cheoah Dam. **Caution:** there is a very steep downhill just before the bridge.
26.2	↑	Pass swinging bridge over Cheoah River and under large green water pipe carrying water from Lake Santeetla.
26.5	←|	Turn **left** on Yellow Creek Road.
34.1	↑	Start very steep climb up to Yellow Creek Gap.
35.3	↑	Yellow Creek Gap. Top of steep climb and Appalachian Trail crossing. Road becomes Tuskeegee Road. **Caution:** the next mile is steep downhill with one sharp, hairpin curve!
37.3	↑	Bottom of hill.
38.1	↱(STOP)	Turn right at stop sign onto NC 28.
38.4	|→	Finish at Tuskeegee Baptist Church.

Wayah Gap (p. 68)

0.0		Leave Nantahala Outdoor Center and ride east on US 19/74. **Caution:** US 19/74 has no shoulder and sees heavy tourist traffic.
4.3	↑	Continue **straight**. US 19/74 becomes a 4-lane highway.
7.5	↦	Turn **right** on NC 28 (Bryson City Road).
16.5	↑	Pass Cowee Creek Pottery on the left.
27.9	↑	Enter town of Franklin.
28.6	↱🚦	Turn **right** at traffic light on West Main.
29.1	↗🛑	Bear **right** at stop sign onto Old Murphy Road.
33.6	↦	Turn **right** on Wayah Road.
36.8	↑	Pass USFS Arrowood Glades Campground and Forest District Work Station. Start climb.
42.8	↑	Wayah Gap and top of climb. Its mostly downhill from here back to Nantahala Outdoor Center.
62.1	↱🛑	Turn **right** on US 19/74. **Caution**: US 19/74 has no shoulder and sees heavy tourist traffic.
70.1	↤	Finish at Nantahala Outdoor Center.

Waterrock Knob (p. 72)

0.0	↰🛑	Leave East Elementary and turn left on US 19.
0.7	↦	Turn **right** on Highway 19A and cross river.
2.3	↤	Turn **left** on Shoal Creek Road.
4.6	↱🛑	Turn **right** on 4-lane US 441. **Caution**: US 441 has no shoulder and it does have a curb.
5.8	↤	Turn **left** on Sunset Farm Road.
7.9	↰🛑	Turn **left** at stop sign and at bottom of steep hill onto 4-lane US 74. It has a wide paved shoulder.
18.1	↤	Turn **left** after 2nd Sylva exit onto Steeple Road.
18.3	🛤↱	**Caution:** cross railroad tracks and then turn **right** on Old Highway 19.
18.8	🛤	**Caution:** cross railroad tracks.
19.0	🛤	**Caution:** cross railroad tracks.

Waterrock Knob (continued)

23.0	⊣	Just before 4-lane, turn **left** on Willets Road.
23.6	⊩▧	Turn **right** across railroad tracks onto Park Ridge Road.
24.5	⊣	Turn back to **left**.
		Caution: next 2 miles is a hard-packed dirt road.
26.4	↑	Road becomes paved again.
27.7	↑▧	Pass Balsam Mountain Inn on right.
		Caution: cross railroad tracks.
28.2	↱ YIELD	Turn **right** at yield sign on Candlestick Lane.
28.3	↱ STOP	Turn **right** at stop sign on 4-lane US 74.
28.4	⊩▧	Turn **right** across railroad tracks and wind through Blue Ridge Parkway Work Station up to the Parkway.
28.5	↰ STOP	Balsam Gap. Turn **left** at stop sign on Blue Ridge Parkway. Start 8-mile climb up to Waterrock Knob.
36.7	↑	Waterrock Knob. Elevation 5800 feet. Top of long climb.
41.2	↑	Soco Gap. Cross overpass over US 19.
43.7	↑	Pass spur road to Heintooga Ridge.
		Caution: there are 6 tunnels between here and the end of the Parkway. **A front light and a rear reflector are required to pass through the tunnels.**
54.6	↰ STOP	Turn **left** on US 441 toward Cherokee.
55.0	↑	Leave Great Smoky Mountains National Park.
55.2	⊣	Turn **left** on Big Cove Road.
55.3	↱ STOP	Turn **right** to remain on Big Cove Road.
55.8	↰	Turn **left** onto Aquone Road to bypass main drag through Cherokee.
57.7	↱▯	Turn **right** at traffic light on US 19 and take it up the hill and out of town.
62.5	↑	Pass Highway 19A on left.
63.2	⊩	Finish at East Swain Elementary.